The Broken Spine
Artist Collective

A Collection of
Poetry & Photography

Third Edition

⬛ ≡BROKEN SPINE

The Broken Spine Artist Collective
Third Edition

Art and Literature

ISBN: 978-1-8380407-2-7

@ Paul Robert Mullen & Alan Parry, 2021. All rights reserved.
003

Book and cover design: Andrew James Lloyd
Cover image by Stuart Buck
Twitter: @stuartmbuck

The Broken Spine Artist Collective
Southport / England / United Kingdom
www.thebrokenspine.co.uk
Twitter: @BrokenSpineArts
Instagram: brokenspinearts

'You may encounter many defeats but, you must not be defeated.'

Maya Angelou

Contents

You Can Take Nothing From Me That Death Hasn't Already Got Its Eye On

First I look for straight edges
and corners
then I search out eyes

then faces
then hands
There is solace in making sense of a puzzle

Next I look for lines and patterns
the scarcest shade
the obvious and less obvious features

then pieces that contain more than one colour
or display some detail however small
then those with a change of tone

finally I consider the curved shapes
using trial and error
until eventually the image is complete

It is an exercise in solitude
almost of prayer
irrespective of the final picture

Henry Normal

Any Old Sicilian Street

Just to be perverse, I make a stop
at a quiet, old-fashioned cafe that,
I was cautioned, was "merda"

which translates to 'not the best'.
Gossip, not mafia, is kiss of death
everywhere in the cafesphere.

Coffee divine! And sinfully
yummy apple danish renewed
my faith in that original fruit.

Allan Lake

Poker

We would walk miles on a Sunday night
from Jarrow to Hebburn with next-door-to-nothing
rattling in our pockets.
Coins in the centre of the table–
if you won you took the pot.
I cannot recall ever winning.
There were four of us.
Two are dead.
Now I spread cards on this table,
shuffle them together, let them fall apart.

Tom Kelly

Middle C
(after Room in New York 1932 by Edward Hopper)

nobody can look at yesterday's weather –
only as a whim or a historical detail
each day sheds the last one like an old shell

middle C on the white keys is like
the New York City summer heat – a symphony
of one note with traffic as percussion

of course I never learned to play
and this is the only key I know and seek
when the lid is lifted on this unwanted piano

nobody in the building has ever complained
even if I sometimes reach a crescendo
and descend on the chord I've just made up

it fades slowly in the confines of the room
to a fresh nothing that ascends to our high
ceiling then disperses softly by the window

James Bell

Ghost Coo

She is the ghost of a former goddess
Poetry princess - the giver of oceans
And smiles - beautiful bangs and big-sad-eyes

Took a pill, too many many pills, of so many types
The water brackish, corrosive around her ankles

The imprint of a gun barrel between her worry lines
Like a henna marker - cherry plum circle of her dowry

Gone dry, mists ascending, the virgen no longer -
There was so much to give, to so many - legs open

Arms open; a mind spewing the words which mesmerize -
Entice. Excite. Whom do they excite -

The swirling whorls of
Masculinity - the stoic pillars -

Pillared type of
Matriarchy - and she still coos

Into your ear, late at night
The ticking of the keys - fingernails upon each vertebrae

Tapping out the braille meme for failure - your skin aroused
Your whiskers bristling -

She leaves a smell of must and rot
Almonds... roses.

Winter is coming - and all she can imagine
Is the young turtles dying -

She wears a shawl - and nothing
Else -

In this year which is worsening -

Maybe - she dons an abandoned shell.

Or maybe she chooses to go bare -
Barren. No longer giving, wearing

Nothing at all.

Elisabeth Horan

Do You Remember the Last
Time You Left For Work?

During the first year of the plague
when reflection came as healing
for YouTube snippets on DIY –
repeats of unfunny sit-coms.

Did we see a part of the world die?
when news is muted from the realities -
Do you remember the last time you left for work?

when amber fields did shine with honeysuckle,
spring had invited the ghosts of summer –
to dance along a river of yellow and red sun

caught between the foggy breath in February
& the daylight that rises early in March -
when space and intimacy weren't an issue.

Do you remember the last time you left for work?
before summer and the autumn of a second spike –
it was back to the season of unnatural light -
when acorns scattered again like shattered thick egg shells.

Matthew Duggan

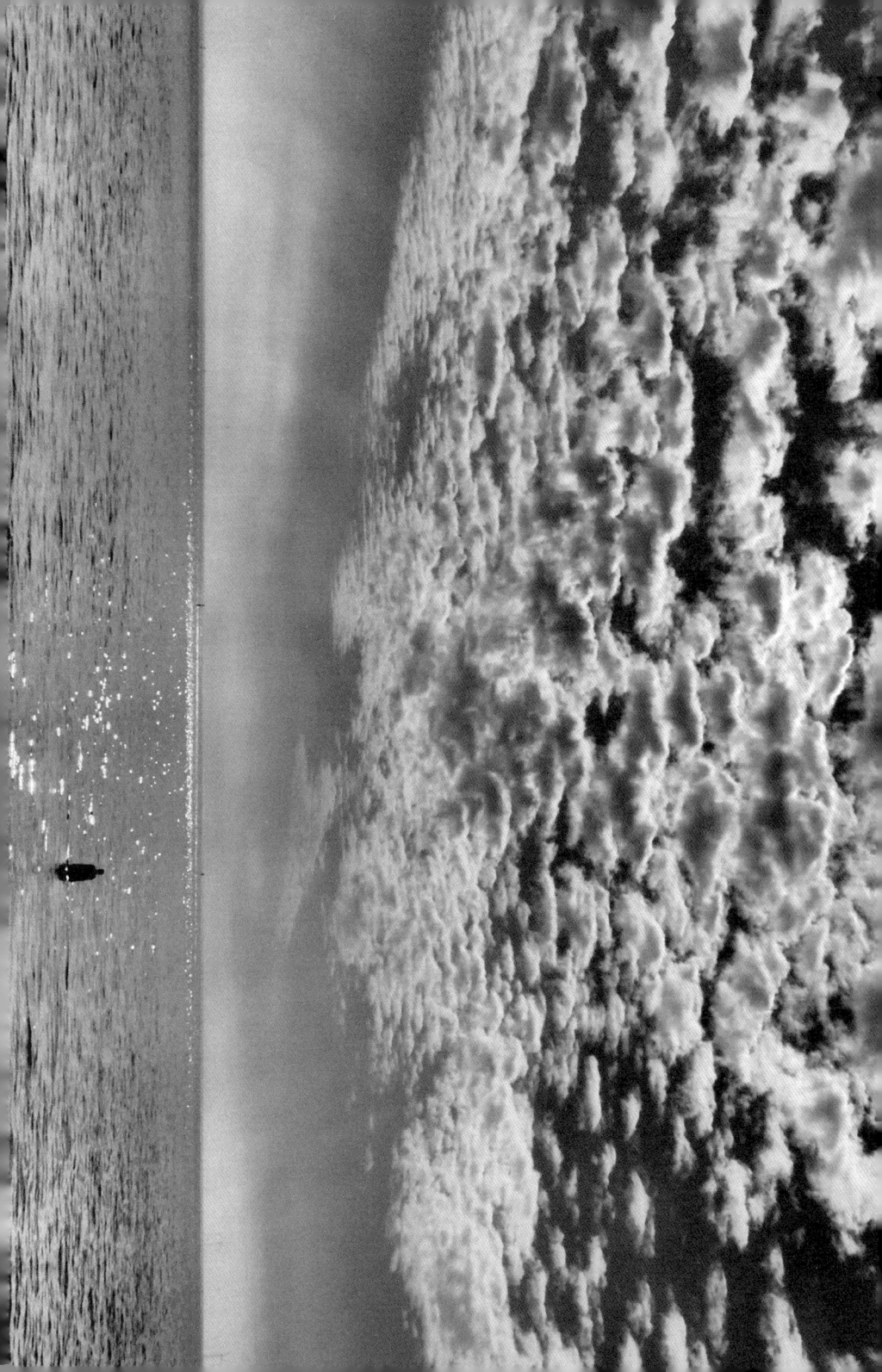

Madame Blavatsky, Queen of Cuffs

Behold, we have before us something unremarkable –
a baby girl, not worth educating, born into corsets

and codes of conduct. Now look at our great Madame,
who took that punch in the stomach and never flinched.

The blows kept on coming – a dour look, two bulging eyes,
an excess of chins – but she stayed on her nimble feet.

Next came the gold ring that had her manacled to a man
more than twice her age. She tore through those bonds

as if they were paper, unlocked the door to the library
and found so many other worlds in those books –

some you can reach by crossing an ocean if you dare,
but others lie back in the unfathomable past or beyond a veil.

Not content to dream, our Madame woke up and went in search
of new gods from the East, who blessed her freedom.

Watch her now, waving her hands as she speaks of spirits;
light fractures through the rubies and garnets on her rings.

Has she travelled to occult lands, conversed with otherwise
mute apparitions? Ladies and gents, we must try to unravel

the conundrum – does she have power beyond the mortal realm?
This much we know: here was a most unpromising woman,

stout and untidy, and she cast her azure eyes across continents,
lived with lovers, smoked cigarettes and hash with abandon,

wrote books as if no one had ever tried to cinch her in. Perhaps
she had dubious morality, but she gave comfort to soldiers

when they needed it most, cured mothers and beloveds
sick with horror at otherwise irreparable loss.

We can't say it was all hokem when she unwound every rope
that tried to bind her, held her breath in the water tank

of whispered gossip and flat accusation, escaped every time
her society tried to strap on a straightjacket.

Zoe Mitchell

God and State

Burnt trees with
burnt leaves in burnt soil.
Observe what man did
with Eden.

We don't take kindly
to rejection it seems
but then neither did
He. Jonah's gnashers
Smote for kicking up a fuss,
Sodom and Gomorrah lost
like so many rotten teeth.
Could you really fault Him
for that? Aren't we the same
as Himself?

He built walls, we build walls.
He demanded blood, we demand blood.
Like Father, like child:
poorly parented,
never taught to share,
prone to tantrums.
Paper or plastic?
Drugs or drink?
The body or the soil?
Semantics.
Why split hairs over our
poison and canvas?

A chain is only as strong
as its weakest link
and our chain has too many
rusted links. It's a pity
they are the ones in charge.
The health service
could use more WD-40.
Now that's a plan
we could all get behind.

A detox of the species.
Just wipe off the top layer.

Rusty people with
Rusty thoughts and rusty morals.
Notice what God does
to people.

Jay Rafferty

Looney Recession

Ah da-
da-
da-
da-
da-
da-
da-that's all folks!

Porky Pig has left the building.
Times are tough.
These days stutters sell less
Than what the butcher pays.

But don't worry!
The show will go on.
It must—
There's no one here
To end it.

Jay Rafferty

1970 Harpurhey is Singing

I took up folk because I knew the stitch of it
the warp and weft of it
the cable knit of it
I sang the songs because
we were warmed by the coal of it
scrubbed by the stone of it
Ate the cold fat of it
Read by the tallow it lit

Because my father sailed ships
and dug earth
and my mother stitched until
her eyes grew buttony
And we drank ale to be rid of it
And we drank ale to be rid of it
And we drank ale to be rid of it
And we drank ale to be rid of it

So, how could I do anything
in this life of blood and bread and war and roses
Save sing folk songs?
In Harpurhey
they were the reason we were born with tongues

Helen Darby

West Pier

There was no grand fire that undid
the western pier. Despite current appearance,
decline was gradual and insistent. Winter
waves scrapping, grabbing handfuls of skin
and hair with each lick since 1975.

This century, someone with a heightened sense
of the theatrical let flames loose, to create
a picture of dramatic death. As ignorant passersby
observe a piece of modern art, filling in
the gaps with convenient truths.

Sarah O'Connor

Lockdown Aftermath - Mike Hindle

The Three Reds

My basket was cottage –
the other two were traditional cob
and white bloomer. First:
Thumbelina. We found a fistful each
of such girls and padded our baskets,
our bras thus. Bluebells, moon-
pennies, the sharp buttery gorse bursts.

The Hag ushered us under her scaly wing.
The Hag taught us to swallow bricks –
red, brown, greyish, rain-slicked.
We could distend our jaws like jungle snakes
and pull out the bricks, lob them
through tower windows or bludgeon
a wolf to death if so required. We could stretch
wolfskin like a tarp and hold court
under the stars of grey hairs, perfectly dry.

We forsook our neatly-healed boots,
all the better for running.
We weren't barefoot for long –
soil, scat, the yolks of the eggs we smashed
in our ritual dances. The Hag was generous,
fed us wild garlic and nettles.
We grew serrated, her happy
bloody grinning knives. Her babes.

Sometimes we would speak in tongues,
our mothers' voices calling us back
or else the moon when the moon is trashed
and shaking the trees hellishly.
The Hag was sometimes a rabbit.
When she died for the final time we buried one foot
and took one each for good luck.
Our baskets were, by now, full:
antlers, bones, thorns, spent ammo, small teeth we found
and knew to hold onto.

We still meet up sometimes, after dark
to hurl bricks at the moon
and show off our latest wolfskins over a frothy glass of red.

Ellora Sutton

Coetus Nervosa

The lady says she has four hours in which to fit
an eight-week anxiety course.

This makes everybody laugh. I eat a tiny twix
from a tin of Celebrations.

Free NHS Health Check

The lady flits about like a red wasp. The man
opposite has tears tattooed beside

his left-eye. His arms are covered in dragons.
There's a cupboard full

of Celebrations tins and a poster that reads,
'Not all stars belong in the sky.'

I CAN YES I CAN

The dragon-sleeved man tells us he
cries at night. I wrote

on the feedback form: 'A bit quick but it
was nice to see others struggling.'

Liam Hayes

The Cafe on the Pass

This is a requiem for a cafe,
and not for the Parisian kind,
all red wine, jazz and candlelight,
but the cafe on the pass,
an old-school-bikers' haunt
of tea-urn fug and butty sweat,
found where the old high road
slashes at the back of the Pennines
in between the miners' cairns
and so much in its elements
that one time I was doing forty-five
and halfway across the yard
until the spray of the guttering
flagged up how I had lost my way.

Another day, a blizzard night,
I found a gritter steaming
metallic vitality into the storm
and it was no choice at all
to wait to follow it down
with flashing lights a safe hypnosis
when summer days are far away
and I wept in exile when I heard
that it was in such a tempest
that the fire burned all night,
the smoke lost within the wind,
angry flames concealed by cloud,
and if I have rightly heard the tale
of the eco-palace now proposed,
while snapshot tourists may rush by,
with the kitchen staff long gone
and the older bikers out of place
there will be little carried over
and too much still left unsaid.

Laurence Morris

Figs

one night – thirsty,
half-awake & stiff

i stumbled naked to
the kitchenette –
outside – tarnished yellow
streetlights
uttered hot-jazz nonsense

slouched over in the
armchair – in
raven silence – the lodger
quaffed port from the bottle –
he didn't notice

i stood for a moment
eating figs from the refrigerator

wordless, i grabbed two glasses from a
shelf & sat cross-legged
on the rug –

he poured us each a dram –
outside silver rain fell harder

i thought you were out tonight
i said

she never showed
he replied

i'm sorry...

we sat up
talked about women & love
until the bottle was
empty & the lodger's eyes dropped
like curtains

Downtown - Victor Hugo Cardoso

Alan Parry

22

Grounded

From my desk,
six horizons:
sky, Somerset, sea,
far field,
meadow, then lawn,
swallow-stitched together.
*
Upstairs, there's laughter on the radio,
a comic entertains empty rooms.
Downstairs I doodle blank pages while
wet dogs
snooze.
Across the hall, my son's wheelchair creaks
as he heaves himself onto his bed.

The trees
breathe.
*
At first a still focus
on the lawn
blackbird is subject to

gravity

then a flurry
a fuss of wings
a shimmering reappearance
closer

his tail flutes upwards
and
(gymnast)
he regains balance.
*
A sudden cannonade of birds outside.
Exploded out of the kitchen
I'm in the ring, can smell the sawdust, see
Red Indian tail feathers,

a clown's yellow stockings,
the swallows trapezing their outrage.

Manipulating its prey as it flies,
a silhouette – dark puppeteer –
careers towards the yew's canopy.
Sparrowhawk.

*

Flummeries of pigeons
bully through trees
as I study the heat-warped sky.
A lone bluebottle fumbles at a window.
Above
a mewling buzzard laments its solitude.
Only swallows defy the heat's weight
weaving the loom of horizons,
shuttling between the wefts of the wind,
finding no resistance.

*

Once I dreamed I'd found the secret of flight
but they demanded a demonstration,
proof.
So, I showed them.
Soaring above the rose-covered arches
I looked down –
their open mouths were crimson flowers.

Now turned to stone
I orbit my sun.

The pull of his gravity
allows illusions
of escape

though only
elliptical.

Ellie Rees

I Am Black as Ink

As freedom is declared, hymns high above Jamaican soil,
the mistress orders me to speak, adding please with a rare smile.
Begin when you were caught. Describe it all in detail.

She bends towards the page. Did you run for long?
These words remind me of the dogs chasing through the woods.
They knock me to the ground. An overseer grabs my arms.

What about the chains? How tight were they precisely?
I watch her write it down – the pinch, the burn as shackles clamp
my feet held in a fire at the auction block. Stripped naked

in the blazing sun, men touch me with their sweating hands.
When I beg for mercy, the overseer slaps my face. Stop!
Mistress looks distressed, crosses out a line, blotched ink.

We shan't say you were hit. No bruises in this tale.
My readers want a simple slave lament. Of course, you cried.
Let the tears fall soft against soft cheeks, even if they're black.

I'll write it in first person to make it more acceptable – a damsel
in loose rags till you came to my estate known as safe haven.
This is when I scream out, Rape and more than once.

Your husband is a villain. You were blind to all my shame.
Write that down as well. The truth they say, will set us free.
She waves the page to swot me quiet, but I have a taste for speech.

How dare you steal my life in retrospect, appropriate the pain?
Her eyes grow big to hear these words. She knows I've read her books.
Of course I did, on humid days when you were lost in dreams.

I taught myself to read. It's opened up a world unto itself.
Knowledge set me free so I could tell the truth precisely –
the story of my life, how you slapped me hard on that first day.

She runs at me this time, hand held high. I back towards the door.
My voice rings out, Freedom has arrived when it was always mine.
It's time to tell the truth. My skin is black as ink to write it down.

Jenny Mitchell

Thanking Nan for a Souvenir Christ on the Cross

And now 30 years later,
when still not a prayer

> (except, as respect expects, the Lord's
> at weddings and funerals, and occasionally
> at the last drop of day when bad news has been
> received, or as a gracious plea of mercy
> or safe journey for others, just in case)

has been uttered from my lips,
I carefully unwrap this relic

> (a wooden cross, hand span high, a delicate
> silver battered Christ, the usual pose,
> from Portugal, Lisbon, I think)

retrieved from my sock drawer
and squeeze gently, tightly
to feel the warmth,

> (the blaze of Nan's garden dripping with fuchsias,
> the heat of a conservatory's tomato sun,
> the tick of her oven cooling caramel shortbread,
> the calm of Clayderman ivories on tape,
> the rhythm of her woven necklace)

that my mother still harbours.
Then it returns to safe keeping,
once I'm refilled and remembered,

> (this time to my sewing box, scruffed with time,
> its contents now strewn across the floor,
> as I stitch a dress for my daughter)

to be carefully forgotten again.

Marcelle Newbold

Evening entertainment

After dinner we arranged the guests on the settee and dimmed the lights for the evening entertainment. My father laid me out on the coffee table, placed newspaper on the floor and took a saw to my swollen abdomen. Reaching inside he produced a coat hanger, dinner plate, hammer and nails. It was worth the effort of swallowing and the stomach cramps during tea to see the looks on their faces, and for the glass of milk and two chocolate digestives at bedtime after mother had sewn me up with the itchy black thread.

Patrick Widdess

Foreplay

We broke up over morning tea
overlooking the Adriatic Sea
in a blue cliffside pensione
run by an elderly Croatian man
who spoke broken English.

Her tears slowly slipped
into her delicate teacup
and we agreed to call it quits.
In silence, we ate the dry biscuits
and drank the bitter tea.

Then we burst out laughing
and climbed the creaky stairs
and made love with the window open,
the cool sea air tossing
the thin white curtains.

Alisa K. Moore

White Flag

Between us an Armada of sails
white flags pegged to the washing line
that lassoed the hook hammered into the mortar
splitting our terraced houses.

Gossip high walls
were freshly pointed
on our side alone.
We didn't speak much or
see each other at the library;
the corporation whitewash of our Methodist chapel
clashed with your Sunday Mecca Bingo bus trips.

Your gate stuck and snicked too loud.
Sometimes you sneaked through ours
to gather arms of left out washing
when the rain began to spit
to leave them in the wash house
with the wooden army of my toy soldier pegs.

But Mam said
She never puts them in the bag
and she always leaves the bloody line out.

Steve Harrison

First Time

You come on to me
like autumn evening–

slow, unexpected, warm,
give me just enough

space to say no
or let's wait.

But I don't.
I want to push

into a tangle of sheets
and unintelligible words.

I give you permission
to touch. I am open,

but the limits of female
never occurred to me,

before this. How it feels
to eavesdrop

on a private conversation
between two bodies.

We are alike but not.
There is no bed

without a middle,
where we meet.

Learn a new way
to tell time–your hand

pressing on my neck
means my minute is up,

and you will lose sight
of me and the dark.

You will forget
we were hungry

and did not eat
when we had the chance.

In a moment
you erase my anxiety

as you unzip your jeans,
chase me down, down, down,

and I show you
here is where you are
and this is how I like it.

Sarah Marquez

What do you do in self isolation?

Alone, at night,

I study with devotion the high-pitched
Vernacular of seagulls, so that I, too,
May be pushed by windy waves to hover
Over a mist-covered ocean
And watch from such altitude

The bending horizon of human future;
My notebooks filling with winged
And beaked hieroglyphs furiously
Fluttering in the mind's eye,
Departing the pages - as if alive -

Staining with ink my bedroom walls,
Marking my hands and lips
When I ask them: "What do you know?"
So be it: I will not write or speak words
Other than volatile.

My room becomes an untranslated book.
I am the book: its bird-shaped gospel lives
Through my skin.
Feathery movements and thoughts
Fill my nest of solitude and tremble

In the air, searching balance, taking off
The ground of life as I knew it.
In a whirl of black-inked plumage
I understand this is a language of love.
I am a book I can't read.

What I crave is not transmutation
But the vision of undimmed eyes.
Reborn
I spread my wings and see clearly.
When I jump, I leave the window open.

Maria Popovic

37

Two things I know, Father Byrne

The size of the needle's eye
through which I am observed
will remain unchanged

whether I borrow modesty
from a pencil's nib,
or score my flesh with truths;

so honeyed they carve
contrails in skies
above my gunmetal town.

The length of eternity for you,
who stalks the walled grounds,
stark and forlorn, is equal

to that of my lover who leans
in thorn-threaded hedgerows,
naked as winter's larch,

and waits for me to prick
his sensibilities
with the tip of my tongue.

FEATURED
POET

Morag Anderson

Riding the Slowtrane

When my departure point turns to rust
and the boards on which I sit soften,
I slip the sleeve.

When sheets of rain keep me awake
and my body aches for the arms of sleep,
I lift the needle.

When my temple's shell starts to crack
and my tread-on-water leaves no mark,
I choose revolution.

When I decode the darker phrase
that slays my skin with violet sound,
I escape like bottled light.

When notes, seeded in long play grooves,
smooth the furrows of Trane's black brow,
no sound on Earth is innocent.

FEATURED
POET

Morag Anderson

ok mary

what is it you plan to do with your one wild and precious life?
Mary Oliver

i'll run away / & ride the rollercoaster in blackpool over &
over again till i'm sick / i'll park the car in the middle of the
cul-de-sac like a roundabout / like a glorious monument /
they'll say poor parking / i'll say good / burn the windscreen
note / run a marathon cook a roast paint a room take a lover
take two lovers / take showers in the middle of the day /
sleep / waft in a kaftan / write a poem a novel a play / play
myself / stay up all night debating quantum physics / do the
school run on roller skates make hallucinogenic risotto /
take ecstasy take DMT pick the brains of dead relatives /
paint my face with edible glitter / have someone delicious
lick it off / dance / dive with sharks drive to peru in a cut
& shut limo with a haversack & a hundred close friends in
fancy dress / play progressive house at five am / invite
everyone i ever knew to come & sing karaoke / when people
ask me what i'm up to now i'll tell them / they'll say crazy /
i'll cartwheel away down the road / will live / will live /
somehow

Insane - Victor Hugo Cardoso

Katie Jenkins

40

How Do I Call My Boyfriend in America?

Fourteen, no, thirteen, hugged by desolate New Forest
idle in a dial-up bedroom, stuffed with
$$silver\_wolf\_88$$
and
$$peanutterbutter$$
or
   carazyrobbotee
et al. aliases fermented somewhere between
the names themselves and the person hidden behind so

I melted into foreign web habitat: devouring Marc Bolan melodies,
uploading bare belly for approval and dawdling,
pausing
for similar souls to scurry by when
he, twenty-one, self-edited and charismatic,
scrambled, no, stirred his, I've no doubt,
reheated chat, dripping with accented innuendos
alongside unscrutinised steamed pictures
inciting immature feelings that determined infantile action,
in which after school chats trickled into after bedtime
conversations
where his proclamations were so welcome
it marinated the backdrop of parental war in a vinegar of
dewy-eyed dopamine,
goading me with loyalty and a proclivity for posting presents
of flowers, no, dildos
from, what I now know, was the attic in his mom's
townhouse, where,
with my teenage magnifying glass,
I should have examined the archaic custard curtains he hid
his crow's feet behind,
in a blend of legerdemain and sleight of
hand me the landline, won't you, mom?

My fingertips tap-tapped the keys as softly as sign language
while the house slept with arguments paused
but his demands of
play

fingers
videos
awoke, and so I faded
from the heather carpeted thickets here,
arms linked, boys giggled at, blackberries basketed
descending instead to the metallic cocoon in there,
withdrawn, alone but adored,
'til all that I was, all that I could be was owned by him ---

Where were you --- hurling coffee at each other in the
kitchen?
        Where were you --- or would I have not stopped even if
forbidden?

Overdue internet inspection ensued,
my eyes
grated from squinting at that foggy, scanned polaroid
of an eighties waistcoat as oversized as my gullibility,
the truth laid naked as I had done,
spatchcocked, over fifty times and yes, I counted,
me, not yet seventeen and he, forty-four, a son my age
and all but his surname a lie ---

Thirty, no, twenty-nine, on some crowded Brixton rooftop,
I stare at the cosmos and the sprinkled pin pricks he sees too
and dream of where I would stick
that pin
        prick.

Abi Loughnane

Skeleton Coast

It is the season for bones.
Wind whips high tides
to lash pier and promenade.
Windscreen-wipers
make their voyages –
to fro to fro to fro.

Giants, who bestrode warm
summer days are gone,
replaced by winter-seaside-drab.
Does anyone mourn
their passing? Notice
their disjointed skeletons

laid beside the road in a very
public mortuary? Limbs,
gargantuan in primary colours,
lying in ranks on
miserable ground.
Pleasureland rides.

Resting In Pieces.

Mary Earnshaw

On the Meadow

Are you content?
With all
That can be viewed:
Whittle your conscience
Down to a coin

The clay mountains are
Deceptively
Smooth at a distance,
With a stanza
Rotting in each face of rock.

Can you see the foxglove?
A cure and a toxicity-
The salinity in the flow of
Confluence
Conferring with the carrier pigeons
That fly above.

Flowers hang themselves
And rain on pavements,
Early morning watering.
the innocents we have
Lost-

Pirated from our mothers.
The countryside was abducted
By a temple of factories.
The ferns sticking out of the ruin,
Asking you:
Are you content?

Tallulah Howarth

Cocoon

i speak for the surgeon
who cut into my throat
her snail-steady hand
her burning need for a knife

i speak of our nearness,
the moon-jelly of me
the shark-bite of her
that split open my surface

and cleaved my cocoon
i speak for the butterfly
she took from my neck—
how it died, how it flew

Kate Evans

bones of dogs

the bones of all my dogs
are in the dunes -

all four of them
       with one to follow

salt-water clean
& stripped of marrow

there won't be anymore after that

unless, maybe
they bury me there too

Paul Robert Mullen

Kitchen Storms

I peel potato-moons
and wash them in warm water.

The skin falls into the sink like tea leaves
in the bottom of a chipped china cup –
I try to read my fortune in them,

it paints nothing but dirt.

With this plastic peeler my fingers cramp
but I cannot make a perfect sphere,
only flat tears of translucent skin.

The starch makes snow of the silver sink,
I have lost my way in the kitchen-storm.

When I find myself again
I am shaving potatoes –
creating little, imperfect, moons.

Lizzie Kemball

Editors

Alan Parry is a poet, playwright and poetry editor from Merseyside, England. He is an English Literature graduate and English teacher. Alan enjoys gritty realism, open ends, miniature schnauzers and 60s girl groups. He has previously had work published by *Dream Noir, Streetcake Magazine, Black Bough Poetry, Porridge, Ghost City Press, Anti-Heroin Chic*, and others. He cites Alan Bennett, Jack Kerouac and James Joyce as inspiration. His debut collection, *Neon Ghosts*, is available from The Broken Spine website.

Website: *www.alanparrywriter.com*
Twitter: *@AlanParry83*   *Instagram:*   *@alphapapa83*

Paul Robert Mullen is a poet, musician, lecturer, traveller and sociable loner from Southport, near Liverpool, U.K. Paul has spent a decade gradually moving around the world, having lived and worked in the UK, Australia, China and Spain. Paul enjoys Leonard Cohen, bass guitar riffs, porridge, paperback books with broken spines, and all things minimalist. He is a regular contributor at Marias at Sampaguitas and has published three poetry collections on Coyote Creek Books (San Jose, California): *curse this blue raincoat* (2017); *testimony* (2018); *35* (2018); and a poetry chapbook on Animal Heart Press: *disintegration* (2020).

Website: *www.writenowpress.com*
Twitter: *@mushyprm35*

Guest Reader

Kate Evans is the author of two poetry collections, three novels, a book about queer teachers, and the memoir *Call It Wonder*, which won the Bisexual Book Award for Best Memoir. Her most recent book is *Revolutionary Kiss*, a novel she co-authored with Mary Janelle Melvin under the pen name Mary-Kate Summers. Her poems, essays and stories have appeared in more than 50 publications. She holds a PhD and an MFA. A former university professor in California, she now works as a book coach and editor. She lives half the year in Mexico, and the other half she travels.

Website: *www.kateevanswriter.com*
Twitter: *@kateevanswriter*

Poets

Visit The Broken Spine website's *Artist Collective: Third Edition Spotlight page* for a copy of this directory with clickable links.

thebrokenspine.co.uk/spotlight/tbsac3

Morag Anderson is an emerging Scottish poet. Originally from Govan, she now lives in Highland Perthshire. Dispossession, and the disconnection between people, influences her writing. Her poetry has appeared in *Popshot Quarterly, Skylight 47, Finished Creatures, Fly on the Wall,* and *The Scotsman* as well as several anthologies. She was placed third in The Blue Nib Chapbook VI, shortlisted for the Bridport Poetry Prize 2019, won Over the Edge New Poet and the Clochoderick Poetry Prize. As part of *Hamish Matters*, she performed at St Anza Poetry Festival 2020. She is a member of the poetry collective, Poets Abroad.

Twitter: *@morag_caimbeul*   *Instagram: morag_anderson*

James Bell - is Scottish and now lives in France where he contributes non-fiction and photography to an English language journal. He has published two previous poetry collections: *the just vanished place* (2008) *and fishing for beginners* (2010), both from *tall-lighthouse*. Recently his work was featured in Poetry Kit's *Caught In The Net* series. He continues to publish poetry widely online and in print. He also writes short fiction.

Helen Darby is a queer poet from the North West, Her work explores working class life, layered with histories and love. Her favourite poets are Nigel Blackwell, Ivor Cutler and Jake Thackray.

Website: *helendarbypoetry.com*
Twitter: *@helenlouisedarby*

Matthew Duggan was born in Bristol, and now lives in Newport with his partner Kelly and their cat 'Pablo'. Matt considers himself a left-leaning, working class poet, and his work has appeared in many journals including *Dodging the Rain, The Ghost City Review,* and *Oxford Review.* Matt's debut collection *Dystopia 38.10* (Erbacce-Press) won the Erbacce Prize for Poetry in 2015, and he has a second collection *Woodworm* (2019, Hedgehog Press

Poetry), and a pair of chapbooks *One Million Tiny Cuts* (Clare Song Birds Publishing House) and *A Season in Another World* (Thirty West Publishing House) available. Matthew is presently working on his third full length collection.

Mary Earnshaw lives between England's north-west coast and the Lancashire mosslands. Inspired by the natural world, physics and the cosmos, she is also a keen observer of human behaviour. Her poetry can be found in Black Bough's two *Deep Time* anthologies and in *Visual Verse*, as well as *The Broken Spine Artist Collective*. Mary has recently begun publishing a series of letterpress-printed short stories and is the author of a crime fiction novel set in Zambia, where she often spends time with her archaeologist husband.

Website: cosiandveyn.co.uk
Twitter: @MaryEarnshaw

Steve Harrison was born in Yorkshire and now lives in Telford. His work has been anthologised in *Emergency Poet* collections, *Wenlock Poetry Festival*, *The Physic Garden*, *Three drops from a Cauldron*, *Pop Shot*, *HCE*, *Poets' Republic* and *Wetherspoons News*. On-line appearances include *Riggwelter*, *Fair Acre Press*, *Poetry Village* and *Poetry on Loan*. He performs across the Midlands and is a previous winner of the Ledbury Poetry Festival Slam.

Twitter: @Stevebudgie64

Liam Hayes is a poet, speculative writer and creator of interactive and experimental fiction. He lives in Eastleigh, England and is currently studying a BA in Creative Writing at the University of Winchester. His poetry is wry and succinct yet can rupture instantaneously into ruminations on the nature of being and the urban landscape as an extension of the interior. Liam is Sartre in the city; Kierkegaard in a kebab house.

Twitter: @liam_hayes   Instagram   lhayeswriter

Elisabeth Horan is an imperfect creature from Vermont advocating for animals, children and those suffering alone and in pain - especially those ostracized by disability and mental illness. She is Editor in Chief at Animal Heart Press, and Co-Editor at Ice Floe Press. She has several chaps and collections out at Bone & Ink Press, Fly on the Wall Press, Cephalo Press, and Animal Heart Press. Her newest collection, *Just to the Right of the Stove*, was released by TwistIt Press, Feb. 2020.

Website: ehoranpoet.com
Twitter: @ehoranpoet

Tallulah Howarth (she/they) is a 19-year-old poet and self-proclaimed 'actorvist' based in the North West. They have previously had publications in Young Identity's *'No Disclaimers'*, *HEBE Poetry Magazine* and *Now Then Magazine*. Last year, they were shortlisted in the top five for the BBC Young Writers' Award, and recently, shortlisted to represent Manchester in the international Slam-O-Vision. Their work is observational, philosophical and politically-motivated.

Twitter: @TallulahHowarth

Katie Jenkins lives in Gloucestershire. She has poetry in print with The Everyman Library in their *Pocket Poets* series and Acid Bath Publishing in their *Wage Slaves* anthology, and forthcoming with The Poetry Bus. She has poems online with *Floodlight Editions* and *Twist in Time*, and forthcoming with Sonic Boom and 8 Poems. Her travel writing about diving with sharks in Fiji has featured in the *Guardian*. She has a creative writing diploma with distinction from Oxford University.

Twitter: @liljenko

Tom Kelly's ninth poetry collection *This Small Patch* has recently been published and re-printed by Red Squirrel Press who also published his short story collection *Behind the Wall*.

Website: tomkelly.org.uk
Twitter: @tomkelly60

Elizabeth Kemball's work has been featured in journals such as: *Black Bough, Ink Sweat & Tears*, and *Iceberg Tales*. Her micro-chapbook was published by *Nightingale & Sparrow Press* in March 2020. She is an Editor & Designer for Re-Side and is currently studying MA Creative Writing at Cardiff University.

Website: lizziekemball.wordpress.com
Twitter: @LizzieKemball

Originally from Saskatchewan, **Allan Lake** has lived in Vancouver, Cape Breton, Ibiza, Tasmania & Melbourne. Poetry Collection: *Sand in the Sole* (Xlibris, 2014). Lake won Lost Tower Publications (UK) Comp 2017 & Melbourne Spoken Word Poetry Fest 2018 & publication in New Philosopher 2020. Chapbook (Ginninderra Press 2020) *My Photos of Sicily*.

Abi Loughnane resides in London, is currently studying writing with the London School of Journalism and is collating her first collection. She has been published in *The Honest Ulsterman*.

Sarah Marquez is based in Los Angeles and has work published and forthcoming in various magazines and journals, including *Capsule Stories, Human/Kind Press, Kissing Dynamite, Sandy River Review* and *Twist in Time Magazine*. When not writing, I can be found reading and sipping coffee.

Twitter: @Sarahmarissa338

Zoe Mitchell is a widely-published poet whose debut collection, *Hag*, was published in 2019 by Indigo Dreams publishing. She graduated from the University of Chichester with an MA in Creative Writing and was awarded a Distinction and the Kate Betts Memorial Prize. She is currently studying for a PhD in Creative Writing, examining witches in women's poetry.

Website: writingbyzoe.com
Twitter: @writingbyzoe

Jenny Mitchell is winner of the Aryamati Prise, the Segora Prize, a Bread and Roses Poetry Award, the Fosseway Prize, joint winner of the Geoff Stevens Memorial Prize 2019 and a 2 times Best of the Net Nominee. Published widely, a debut collection, *Her Lost Language*, is one of 44 Poetry Books for 2019 (Poetry Wales) and a Jhalak Prize #bookwelove Recommendation.

Twitter: *@JennyMitchellGo*

As comfortable in a biker bar as she is in an ashram, **Alisa K. Moore** embraces non-duality as a spiritual practice, and follows the teachings of Amma and Mooji. A blogger, visual artist, amateur poet and essayist, Alisa authored *Behind the Scenes: How the Universe Conspires to Support Us*, a memoir of her early experiences as a psychic-medium. Alisa's essays on a myriad of topics from menstruation to minimalist living have been published on-line by *Miss. Minimalist, Elephant Journal* and *Epochalips*. By day, Alisa has enjoyed a long social services career, much of it advocating for LGBTQ children and families involved in the foster care system. Alisa currently works on a historic 1,600 acre farm nestled in the Santa Cruz foothills, coordinating educational field trips and social justice summer camp for children.

Website: *augustmoonhealing.com*
Twitter: *@alisakmoore*

Laurence Morris is an academic librarian and a fellow of the Royal Geographical Society. As a keen hillwalker, his poetry explores the relationships between people and place.

Website: *shorturl.at/mtDX4*
Twitter: *@ld_morris*

Marcelle Newbold loves poetry as a way of exploring inner spaces, place and inheritance. Her poems have been published in magazines, and in recent anthologies by Wild Pressed Books and Maytree Press. A poetry editor for Nightingale & Sparrow, she lives in Cardiff, Wales, where she trained as an architect.

Website: *poems.sketch31.co.uk*
Twitter: *@marcellenewbold*

Henry Normal is a writer, poet and TV and Film producer and founder of the Manchester Poetry Festival (now the Literature Festival) and co-founder of the Nottingham Poetry Festival. In June 2017 he was honoured with a special BAFTA for services to Television. He co-wrote and script edited the multi-award winning Mrs Merton show, and co-created and co-wrote the first series of The Royle Family. Setting up Baby Cow Productions Ltd in 1999, Henry Executive Produced, and script edited many of the shows of its seventeen year output during his tenure as MD. Highlights of Baby Cow's output during this time include *Philomena* and *Gavin and Stacey*. Henry performs poetry at Literature Festivals around the UK and has ten recent poetry collections out, and one forthcoming in May 2021 on Flapjack Press, *The Distance Between Clouds*.

Website: *henrynormal.com*
Twitter: *@HenryNormalpoet*

Sarah O'Connor is a new writer, working towards a first collection. Originally from the west of Ireland, O'Connor now lives in London, working backstage in theatre and opera. O'Connor's work can be found in *Abridged* magazine and *The Cabinet of Heed*.

Twitter: *@SarahOCwrites*

Maria Popovic is an emerging poet born in Belgrade and raised in Italy. She is currently based in Dublin in pursuit of a PhD in physics at Trinity College. Despite her scientific background, Maria has found comfort in writing. Her poetry has been published in *Ghost City Review, Barren Magazine* and *Collective Realms Magazine*. Her first play was produced as part of TINY PLAYS 24/7.

Twitter: *@mariaminuszero*

Jay Rafferty is an Irishman, an eejit and the Social Media Manager for Sage Cigarettes magazine. You can read his work in the Alcala Review, 3 Moon Mag, Dodging the Rain, Gravitas, Daily Drunk Mag, Capsule Stories and in Broken Spine journal and website.

Twitter: *@Atlas_Snow*

Ellie Rees is an internationally-minded, award-winning writer who writes across many genres including poetry, creative non-fiction and memoir. Her work is widely published in various journals including: *New Welsh Review, Poetry Wales, Cabinet of Heed, Black Bough Poetry* and *The Lonely Crowd.* She has a PhD in Creative Writing from Swansea University. Ellie's first collection of poetry, Ticking, will be published in 2021 by The Hedgehog Poetry Press.

Twitter: *@ellierees23*

Ellora Sutton is a Creative Writing MA student from Hampshire. Her work has been published by *Poetry Birmingham Literary Journal, Mookychick, Young Poets Network,* and *Poetry News,* amongst others. She won the inaugural Poetry Society and Artlyst Art to Poetry Award. Her debut chapbook is out now from Nightingale & Sparrow.

Website: *ellorasutton.com*
Twitter: *@ellora_sutton*

Patrick Widdess lives in Norwich. His poetry has appeared in publications including *The Guardian, The Interpreter's House, Ink, Sweat and Tears, Cake, Agenda* and *Waitrose Weekend.* He hosts the podcast Poetry Non-Stop: poetrynonstop.com

Website: *patrickwiddess.co.uk*
Twitter: *@patrickwiddess*

Artists and Photographers

Stuart Buck is a writer and artist currently living between the UK and Colorado. When he is not creating himself, he runs the fictional online newspaper *The Bear Creek Gazette*.

Twitter: @stuartmbuck   @bcgazette

Bill Bulloch is a photographer and poet, whose work has been featured on *Zimzalla, Dock Road Press* and *Nightjar Press*. Bill lives in West Lancashire and works for Edge Hill University.

Website: nightsfullnine.blogspot.com
Instagram: wotanicus

Victor Hugo Cardoso is a Brazilian artist who seeks to portray the various aspects of man's introspection in the modern world, his loneliness, pain and resignation. His art, often self-referential, brings his own emotional charge pictured in solitary figures overlapped on colored backgrounds, in his simple compositions highlighting lines and geometric shapes.

Instagram: victorhc.art

Ron Davies is a retired commercial photographer who loves to record art, nature and landscape in images and words.

Twitter: @RonDaviesPhotos

Martins Deep (he/him) is a Nigerian poet, photographer, & student of Ahmadu Bello University, Zaria. He is passionate about documenting muffled stories of the African experience in his poetry & visual art. He was the winner of the August/September edition of the Brigitte Poirson Poetry Prize, and also a semi-finalist for the Jack Grapes Poetry Prize 2020. His creative works have appeared, or are forthcoming on *The Roadrunner Review, Barren Magazine, Chestnut Review, Mineral Lit Mag, Agbowó Magazine, Writers Space Africa, Inklette, Suburban Review, The Quills, Typehouse Literary Magazine, The Alchemy Spoon, Dream Glow, The Waxed Lemon, Kalopsia Literary Journal, Lumiere Review, Variant Literature*, & elsewhere. He is also the brain behind Shotstoryz Photography.

Twitter: *@martinsdeep1*   *Instagram:* *deep_martins*

Owner and graphic designer at Clearcut Derby, **Mike Hindle** is a creative with a passion for variety. As a side-project, photography offers a much-needed escape from the studio. Although people sometimes feature in Mike's work, he loves nothing more than capturing desolate and abandoned scenes.

Twitter: *@MikeHindle*

Arin Paul Kapur. Enigmatic. Charismatic. Passionate. Lover of life and all truth in it. UK Based visual artist.

Twitter: *@arunkapur333*

Thank You

A special thank you to all of The Broken Spine Family, whether you be a contributor to the Artist Collective, a patron or sponsor, or a customer. Anne Maguire, Eliot North, Mary Jaimes-Serrano and all our other patrons who wish to remain anonymous, we salute you.

A further thanks should go to Andrew James Lloyd who has worked tirelessly on each of our publications, our website, and on all the other design work he has undertaken, and for the advice offered.

In tribute to the memory of Michael Lockwood, founder of *Southport Bijou Cinema*.